Presented to:

_____

From:

_____

Date:

_____

*The greatest medicine is
a true friend.*

Sir William Temple

kisses

from a

Friend's Heart

Heartwarming Messages
That Encourage & Inspire

HOWARD BOOKS
A DIVISION OF SIMON & SCHUSTER
New York   London   Toronto   Sydney

Our purpose at Howard Books is to:
- *Increase faith* in the hearts of growing Christians
- *Inspire holiness* in the lives of believers
- *Instill hope* in the hearts of struggling people everywhere
  Because He's coming again!

Published by Howard Books, a division of Simon & Schuster, Inc.
1230 Avenue of the Americas, New York, NY 10020
www.howardpublishing.com

HOWARD
BOOKS

ISBN 978-1-4767-3813-0

10 9 8 7 6 5 4 3 2 1

HOWARD and colophon are registered trademarks of Simon & Schuster, Inc.

Manufactured in the United States of America

For information regarding special discounts for bulk purchases, please contact: Simon & Schuster Special Sales at 1-800-456-6798 or business@simonandschuster.com.

Project developed by Bordon Books, Tulsa, Oklahoma
Project writing and compilation by Christy Phillippe in association with Bordon Books
Edited by Chrys Howard
Cover design by Greg Jackson, Thinkpen Design

Introduction

A kiss. It's short. Sweet. And packed with love. That's what *Kisses from a Friend's Heart* is all about. Each page of this book is a message straight to your heart from mine, filled with joy and gratitude for the wonderful friend that you are. As you read, I hope you'll discover how very special both you and your friendship are to me.

A friend loves at all times.

PROVERBS 17:17 NIV

It's so important in life to have a few
special friends,

you know, the ones who come in

when others go out,

who bring sunshine and joy,

a listening ear,

and a box of chocolates

they can't wait to share.

You are that irreplaceable
friend to me!

You bring a smile to my face

on the bluest of days,

and you always know how to make the ordinary extraordinary!

You are a beautiful person—

inside and out—

and my life is so much richer
with you in it.

Your kindness . . .

your loyalty · · ·

your hilarious sense of humor . . .

and your unwavering faith in me

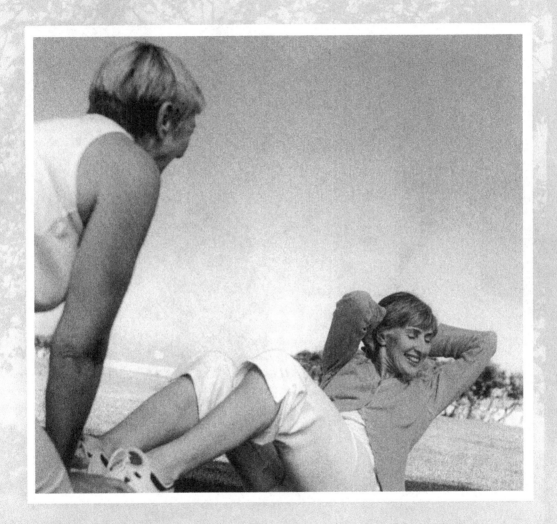

all make you one of my dearest,
most cherished friends.

You always seem to know
just what I need:

you hug me when I'm sad . . .

you hold my hand when
I'm scared . . .

you give honest, heartfelt
advice (even if I don't
want to hear it) . . .

and you even help me
get out of sticky situations.

But you're there for me in the
good times too.

Who else could make me laugh
until my stomach hurts?

You cheer for me
when I reach my goals,

and we celebrate triumphs together,

great and small!

You accept me for who I am . . .

my good side . . .

my bad side . . .

and everything in between.

You make me want to be
a better person,

more adventurous...

more willing to give
of myself . . .

more grateful for the gifts

I have been given—

especially for you!

You are one in a million!

You always make time for me

no matter how busy you are.

And whatever we do together . . .

meeting for gelato on the go . . .

having lunch at our

favorite restaurant . . .

spending an afternoon

at the mall . . .

or a relaxing night of girl talk
in our pajamas . . .

it's guaranteed to be fun—

especially watching that chick flick
we are both dying to see!

We both know how to
appreciate the important
things in life:

the perfect pair of sunglasses . . .

the perfect pair of shoes . . .

and the perfect pair
of friends!

When we aren't together,
I miss you—

but we always pick up right
where we left off,

sharing our hopes,

our fears,

our memories,

and our hearts.

We all have friends who come
and go in our lives—

but the ones who stay

are the ones who count.

It has been one of the
greatest joys of my life

to call you my friend.

LOOK FOR THESE BOOKS

Kisses of Comfort

Kisses of Encouragement

Kisses from a
Mother's Heart

Kisses of Love

Kisses from a
Sister's Heart

HOWARD BOOKS
A DIVISION OF SIMON & SCHUSTER
New York   London   Toronto   Sydney

Printed in the United States
By Bookmasters